Wordflirt's
How to Become a Social Media
Content Machine

*Wordflirt's Guide to Cranking out KILLER Content to
Grow Your Business*

By

Claudia M. Loens

ISBN: 0989060101
ISBN-13: 978-0-9890601-0-3

DEDICATION

I am so blessed to have a loving, supportive husband and four wonderful daughters. Eddie, my husband, is the quiet, loyal strength powering my dreams. He continues to tell me to "go for it" and applauds even my smallest accomplishments. It took a long time to find him, but ever since our journey began together, my life has been happier than I thought could be possible.

My girls keep me on my toes and remind me of why my dreams are so important. Each of them is an amazing human being that I would love to know even if they weren't my family. When it is time for them to begin their journeys, I want them to have dreams that know no bounds. It is because of them that I am able to follow *my* dreams and I want to instill in them the ability to follow theirs as well.

I couldn't have asked for a better family. They inspire me in everything I do. Without their support, this book would not be possible. So I dedicate it to Eddie, Summer, Madalyn, Theresa and Abigail. I love you all so much.

CONTENTS

ACKNOWLEDGEMENTS

I am pleased to acknowledge my exceptional business coaches – Jim Alvino, Reggie Batts and Michele Peters. First of all, Jim is not only a fantastic business coach, but we share a passion for the Law of Attraction. His business acumen coupled with the proper mindset and encouragement truly helps me to push through the tough aspects of being an entrepreneur. Reggie Batts, in my book, is a genius mindset coach that knows all the right questions to ask to keep me on track. He doesn't let me get caught up in my own excuses and, with kindness, points out challenges that I need to address. And finally, Michele Peters holds me accountable for all of my commitments. She is there when I need resources and to answer questions. These three coaches have helped me make my dreams a reality. Our sessions are filled with information, powerful discoveries and a whole bunch of laughter.

It was several years ago that I learned about Kate Buck, Jr.'s social media training program, Let's Get Social. I eagerly enrolled in the course and proceeded to be wowed by Kate! Her training program was designed to help people like me to build a social media consulting business, complete with all the instruction and tools. Her spunky nature kept the learning process fun and interesting. Meeting her in person twice after that made me an even bigger fan. But when she so generously offered to write the foreword for my book, I was ecstatic and very honored. A special thank you to her! **www.kbjonline.com**

Another spunky teacher that I follow is Jo Barnes. Her Social Networking Academy was another learning resource that made a huge difference in my business. She continues to provide news, updates and learning opportunities to people like me so that we don't have to go scrounge for the information ourselves. She's awesome. www.jobarnesonline.com

And to the many family members, friends and colleagues that have been so supportive over the years – I thank you from the bottom of my heart.

FOREWORD

As the Founder and CEO of KBJOnline, I have trained tens of THOUSANDS of social media managers and helped build and manage social media campaigns for hundreds of businesses for over the last four years. I am often a regular speaker at business conferences on the topic of Social Media. One of the biggest things that both business owners and social media managers struggle with is...

"HOW and WHERE do I not only FIND, but also CREATE original compelling content that will grow my business and my bottom line?"

The truth is, as a business owner, you have an area of expertise and most likely, it is NOT creating social media content. The best use of your time and focus should be spent on running those aspects of your business.

Outsourcing your social media is one way to handle this dilemma, but that can be somewhat tricky. The best use of your resources would be to find a master who knows the main aspects of social media, which include:

- Managing your social profiles
- Creating compelling content that converts your reader into a buyer
- And positions it on social media so that search engines love it (SEO/SMO)

It is difficult to find such a person who knows all of these aspects and when you do, they are in high demand, which can be very expensive!

In "How to Become a Social Media Content Machine" Claudia Loens teaches you how you (yes, YOU) can create awesome content that will showcase you as a Thought Leader in your industry and grow your target audience.

Sometimes creating social media content can be easier than you think. Imagine putting on magical (rose colored!) content glasses that help you to suddenly see a content rich world. Now, everywhere you turn, you see opportunities for business related items to share on social media. Like taking a picture of the new product in your store that you had not considered sharing before. Or an article that you read and realize that you could share the ideas with your audience in your own words and context. Or a customer that is telling you how great you are – and you whip out your smart phone and record it to share on YouTube.

When you put on these magical content glasses, your entire perspective changes so your daily activities become fodder for your social media marketing and it becomes second nature! This is a concept that I would love to see every business owner develop for themselves and their team members.

As you know, in every business, it is crucial that you set up systems to help you perform regular duties in the most efficient way possible. With your new magical glasses, you will see content everywhere and you need a system to help you aggregate and disseminate your abundance of ideas. By breaking down the process into actionable steps, Claudia takes the overwhelm out of content creation by teaching you how to develop your own system. She helps you tap into your knowledge, available resources and tools to develop a solid content strategy, with a system to go with it.

And for my social media students – if you're looking to expand your social media business so that you can offer content creation as a service, this guide will help you do exactly that. When you become one of the masters that I mentioned previously, who offers all aspects of social media, you become more valuable to your clients and you can charge more. AND, you will help your clients to land bigger clients too.

The fact is, most social media trainers, including me, don't include instruction on how to create social media content, for one reason or another. But once you are up and running on the social media platforms and want to take it to the next level, how do you do that?

I'm really pleased that there is finally a comprehensive resource available for my clients and students to help them generate content that will build their businesses by utilizing the gigantic power of social media.

Kate Buck, Jr
Founder and CEO of KBJOnline, Social Media Consultant, Author, Speaker and Trainer
www.kbjonline.com

INTRODUCTION

When you think about it, social media has not been around for very long. And yet, people have flocked to it like crazy. I remember back in the early 2000s the cool new term people were using was to "Google" something. Now, it seems like everywhere I go I hear people saying "I Facebooked it" or some such term as if it is a true verb! (I wonder if it will end up in the dictionary?!)

The statistics are staggering:

✓ Facebook now has **1 BILLION** users
✓ YouTube has **800 Million** users
✓ Twitter has **500 Million** users
✓ LinkedIn has **200 Million** users
✓ Pinterest has **107 Million** users
✓ Pinterest has **107 Million** users
✓ Google+ has **100 Million** users
✓ Instagram has **100 Million** users

According to the Facebook numbers, *one in every seven people* has a Facebook account worldwide.

What this tells me, is that there is no longer a need to define and explain what social media is. Chances are that if you're reading this book, you are already familiar with what it is and now you want to improve your following and have it affect your bottom line. It is one thing to start tweeting or advertise your business on a Facebook page. It is quite another to attract the right kind of followers that will buy from you!

You are probably wondering who I am and why I'm writing this book. I have been a hobby writer my whole life and in 2008, I took my craft on-line. I've written ebooks, blogs, articles and presentations. A couple of years ago, I began taking courses on Social Media management and have since come to manage the social media presence of various small to mid sized businesses. In addition, I was a high tech recruiter in Silicon Valley up until 2012, whereby I used social media to help organizations recruit quality talent.

Today, my company, Wordflirt, writes content for businesses, designs WordPress websites and helps companies with their social media strategy.

I recognize that social media is a moving target, constantly morphing and growing. But I believe that the basics of creating awesome content will always remain a strong foundation despite any changes to the venues.

This is not a "how to set up your social media" book. In this book, you will learn how to determine who your target audience is and how to create content that attracts them to your social media sites. If you are interested in keeping up with the trends and to get tips on social media, follow my blog at **www.wordflirtsocialmedia.com**.

Now, let's get started!

Chapter 1
Why Content Should Matter to You

> ✓ **FACT:** Every minute of the day 100,000 tweets are sent
> ✓ **FACT:** Every minute of the day 684,478 pieces of content are shared on Facebook
> ✓ **FACT:** Every minute of the day 2 million search queries are made on Google*

I love Facebook! I started out using it for personal reasons a few years ago. Being a busy mother of four, entrepreneur and writer, I found that I didn't have time to stay in touch with old friends across the US. So I posted things about my life and read things about my friend's lives. Facebook allowed me to connect in a way I could not before.

At first, I didn't understand when I saw my friends "like" things. I remember first seeing one of my friends becoming a "FAN" and "liking" JCPenney. I thought it was kind of weird. I mean, sure you like to shop there, but why would you announce it to your network of friends? So I looked up JCPenney's fan page and saw that they posted interesting stuff about fashion, shopping, deals and more. I decided to be weird too and I "liked" the page.

The next thing I knew, JCPenney's updates showed up in my news feed. Whenever they posted something, I didn't have to go find it – it came to me in my news feed. All of my friends would see this update too if I was on their news feed. At the time, I didn't understand the value of that for JCPenney.

What it Means to go "Viral"
The value of this type of spreading the word for JCPenney – or any business that you "like" is huge! Imagine if my network is 200 people. They've now advertised not only to me, but to my 200 friends without doing anything else. Perhaps a curious few will click on one of their posts and "like" them too. Soon their reach would include their whole network also. That is the beauty of Facebook for business!

The other social media networks are similar in nature. Twitter is a micro version of blogging – or sharing your thoughts, opinions, news and product information. YouTube is the video version of this phenomenon and Pinterest is the photo version.

When one person shares with their network, then another shares with their network and so on, this is called going "viral". It takes on a life of its own and soon, if you have good content, the number of viewers grows like crazy. Say you are a national retailer like JCPenney – wouldn't you want that for your business? And if you're just a mom-and-pop joint, wouldn't you want it for *your* business too?

You can do far more FREE advertising with social media than you can with a single, expensive ad in a paper or on TV or radio. You can also pay to get targeted advertising, but that is not what this book is teaching you.

Content that Gets Your Attention

So what makes a person want to follow or "like" a business page? Here are *my* top five reasons for "liking" a page:

1. *Educational posts.* Short, but interesting and relevant posts that teach me something or remind me of something are good. Even a simple "did you know..." statement will stimulate my interest. The result..."LIKE".
2. *Humor.* I am a very busy person, but just like most people, I always have time for a chuckle or outright belly laugh! I love nuggets of humor. Recently images of funny sayings have been popular. I like the brevity of delivering funny sound-bites like this, but all humor – when tasteful – is good to me! The result..."LIKE".
3. **Positive quotes.** Like humor, reading a quick positive quote to pick me up is always welcome. Sometimes, it gets me thinking for the rest of the day! The result..."LIKE".
4. **Photos of products, people and events.** I don't mind reading about the news from a business that I follow as long as it's balanced with other information. The result..."LIKE".
5. *Deals or Coupons.* I will certainly "like" a page if the reward is a coupon or discount! Who isn't looking for a good deal? The result... "LIKE".

On the flip side, just as easily as I have "liked" pages because they are interesting to me, I have equally "unliked" them when I don't like the content. Frankly, I'd rather someone post less frequently and post something interesting, than to post a bunch of garbage fifteen times per day!

Dislike

Here are my top five reasons for "un-liking" a Facebook page:

1. *A business that only posts about themselves.* I want to be entertained, educated or intrigued by what I see on Facebook. When the only thing a business does is advertise their wares, I get tired of it. The result... "UNLIKE".
2. *Content that's not relevant to me.* Similar to businesses that only post about them, if whatever topic they are posting is not relevant to me, I'm not interested, nor do I have the time to sift through it. The result ..."UNLIKE".
3. *Posting way too often.* Some businesses think that more is better and will put many posts on their page daily. Frankly, I don't want them clogging up my newsfeed. The result... "UNLIKE".
4. *Posting inappropriate content.* An occasional opinion or stance on a controversial topic is ok with me. But when a business tries to shove something down my throat – such as political or religious views, I don't like it. The result... "UNLIKE".
5. *Constant re-posts and article sharing.* Sharing something that resonates with their customer base, such as another person's post or article is one thing that should be incorporated into a social media strategy. But if that's the only strategy the business has for their Facebook pages, I'm not interested. It doesn't tell me anything about them, their business, their values, their personality or add value to me. The result ..."UNLIKE".

The bottom line is that if you are trying to grow your business by increasing your valued followers, you don't want them to hit that "unlike" button!

If your audience is broad, then the reasons for following or unfollowing a business will also be broad as well. Now, take a moment to ask yourself what makes you "like" and "unlike" a business?

The Value of Content

If case you didn't notice, each of the reasons above is related to the content that is posted. If you run a business and you are eager to grow it, then whatever you post on social media could either support that endeavor or hurt it. Taking the time and energy to craft your content is worth it in the end.

A Word About SEO

Have you heard the term "SEO"? Do you know what it means? Well, many people do not. SEO is simply "Search Engine Optimization". Every single thing you post on the Internet is searchable! So whenever you post on your social media sites, someone out there can and is searching for it, so plan for this when you work on your content!

Recently, a similar term popped up called "SMO" or "Social Media Optimization". Social media has become such a major online force, that it is close to garnering more search opportunities than Google! Therefore, what you post on your social sites is more important now than ever before.

To maximize Search Engine Optimization and Social Media Optimization, you have to put yourself in the shoes of your follower. Figure out what things they are searching for on the Internet and then match up the words you use in your posts to the words they use to search. There are gobs of books, articles, videos and experts out there that can teach you these skills. If you are a beginner, my advice to you is to read an article or two, but don't get hung up on doing it perfectly. Being aware that your subjects are searchable and trying to use keywords when posting is a good place to start. You can determine what your keywords are by utilizing the free tool called Google Keywords.

Now let's get started on YOUR strategy for great social media content!

* Social Media facts provided by www.thesocialskinny.com

Chapter 2
Your Target Audience

> ✓ **FACT:** 83% of users want deals & promotions
> ✓ **FACT:** 58% of users want exclusive content
> ✓ **FACT:** 55% of users want feedback on new products*

Whenever I work with a new client, the very first thing I ask them, is "Who are you trying to reach?" To me, knowing your target audience is a CRITICAL piece of the Social Media puzzle. Without knowing whom you are trying to reach, you could spend time and energy creating great content for your social media campaigns, only to fall short of any real success. By determining your target audience before generating any content, you will save yourself time in the long run and have a far greater chance of accomplishing your social media goals – to get more customers!

So before we create fabulous content, let's take a step back and discuss your target audience.

Defining Your Ideal Customer

Do you know who your ideal customer is? If you have a business plan, you are probably keenly aware of the demographics of your ideal customer. But if you're just starting out, then you may not have thought this part through yet. Here are some questions you can ask to help define who your ideal customer is:

- What are you selling? Is it a product or a service? Is your selling venue a website or brick-and-mortar business?

- What is your business philosophy, vision and mission? Every business should have these. Similar to determining your social media objective, you need to define your business philosophy, vision and mission as early as you can. This will shape just about everything you set out to do when acquiring new customers and building your bottom line.

- What are the demographics of the typical buyer of your product or service? Things to consider are age, sex, marital status, education, income level, sexual orientation, family status, religion and any other interest that is relevant to your business.

- How much time does your ideal customer spend on Social Media? (There are demographics for this if you do a Google search.)

- What problem, discomfort, need or pain are you solving for with your product or service?

- Who makes the buying decision? If your company is a B2B, then what areas of the company to whom you are selling, make the decision to buy your product or service? Is the Finance team involved? Executives? Or are you a B2C and your buyer is a mom or college student?

- What do you like about your ideal customer? What makes the interaction or experience "*ideal*"?

- What about your nightmare customer? You should define this also. You know the disclaimer "we reserve the right to refuse service to anyone"? Knowing who you DON'T want to do business with is just as important as knowing who you do!

Once you have answered all of these questions for yourself, you should have a pretty good idea of who your ideal customer is.
Congratulations! You also now know who your target audience is!

Determine What Your Target Audience Wants

Now that you know who your target audience is, you must really step out of your own shoes and into theirs. By thinking like your customer, you can develop high quality content that appeals to them and is not just serving you.

For example, if you own a pet store, then posting information about great deli sandwiches, is probably *NOT* going to resonate with your target audience. A better idea, would be to list delis in your area that have outdoor seating so your dog lovers can sit outside with their companion. This has more value to your target audience and will likely attract more dog lovers.

So with your target audience in mind, what information can you post that not only reflects their interests, but also shows your business as an expert resource for their needs? Create categories that reflect areas of interest to your target audience. Let's brainstorm this one, using the pet store as an example...

Areas of Interest – Pet Store
- Tips on how to care for animals
- Safety for animals and their owners
- Animal trends
- History, facts and news relating to animals
- Funny animal stories and photos
- Articles on how to pick the perfect pet, train your dog, name your new pet and facts about specific animals
- Proper diet for pets
- Animal rights
- Accessories, clothing and "bling" for toy dogs
- Health benefits to owning pets
- Cute pet videos
- Nutritional information on popular pet foods
- Recipes for homemade dog or cat food
- Local information relating to pets – pet friendly parks, stores, events, etc

I don't own a pet store, so this is clearly not a comprehensive list. But do you see how easy it is to determine areas of interest that appeal to your ideal customer? Of course, it's ok to throw in a random shout out to your local team or something more personal to you, the owner (we'll get to that later!). But mostly, think about what *YOUR* audience wants and needs that will improve their experience and their lives.

Take some time to write your list for your business. Keep coming back to it over the next few days or weeks to fine-tune it. Remember, much the way social media is evolving, so is your target audience and the information that we have available to us. Don't become so set on your list that you don't see new opportunities to "share" in the future!

Knowing and understanding your target audience is the launching pad for creating social media content that attracts more followers and helps to grow your business.

Use the worksheet on the next page to brainstorm your list.

*Social media facts provided by www.thesocialskinny.com

Wordflirt Worksheet #1
Determine What Your Customers Want

Using the blank lines below, write down all the different ideas you have for creating topics that interest and add value to your customer. Use these questions to help you trigger ideas:

What does my customer have in common with my business or industry?
What does my customer NEED to know to make them better?
What does my customer WANT to know to make them better?
What does my customer like to do?
Where do my customers hang out?
What problems do my customers have?
What questions can I answer for my customers?

_____

_____

_____

_____

_____

_____

_____

_____

_____

_____

_____

_____

_____

Chapter 3
The Blueprint to Creating Balanced Content

✓ **FACT:** 25% of Small to Medium sized businesses DON'T have a social media strategy

✓ **FACT:** Over 50% of workers *over* age 50 use social media every day at work

✓ **FACT:** 77% of B2C companies have acquired customers from Facebook vs. 42% of B2B*

Now that you know the value of content and you have identified your target audience, it's time to give them what they want! In my mind, content can be broken down into three categories:

1. Educational
2. Entertainment
3. Company Promotion

The way you decide to break it down for your business is highly determined by your target audience. For instance, if you are an alternative medicine practitioner, your audience is likely to want more educational content. While, if you're a nightclub, the majority of your content will be entertainment. You will have to think about this as you begin to formulate your strategy for posting balanced content.

Each category can and should be used for every business when determining your strategy for social media. The categories are the blueprint for getting started. Let's delve a little deeper into each so that you can decide for yourself what balanced content looks like for your business.

Educational Content

I hope that you don't think educational equals boring! Educational information can be as light and fun as it is dry and boring. It's up to you to decide how to deliver it in the way that pleases your target audience.

The first thing you need to ask is, "What is my target audience interested in learning that relates to my field or industry?"

Let's use a residential real estate business in this example. In this business, you have two types of potential clients – a buyer and a seller. And let's say you really wish to grow your "first time buyer" client base. There is a huge opportunity to use social media to educate your ideal client.
Here is a list of educational topics that you could craft into social media content:

- How to improve your credit
- What are the steps to buying a home?
- What type of home insurance will I need?
- How does a mortgage work?

- How to select a realtor
- What you need to know as a first time buyer
- Why a home inspection is critical
- Best neighborhoods for schools
- What all the closing costs mean to your bottom line

This is just a small sampling - the list could go on and on. The idea is to put yourself in their shoes and come up with topics that would enrich them in your field of expertise.

By addressing these topic areas, you are showcasing your expertise and your audience will see you as a thought leader in your industry.

Entertainment

Entertainment is the cornerstone of social media! Your target audience probably values this above the educational, because that is why they are visiting social media sites to begin with – to be entertained. I call this putting the "social" into social media. So how can you use this to your business advantage?

As in educating your ideal client, you should brainstorm a list of topics that would be both relevant to your business and relevant to your client. I break it down into three categories:

1. Social topics that relate to your industry
2. Social topics that relate to the mass population.

3.   Events and subjects that everyone relates to

Let's look at each of these more closely.

Social topics that relate to your industry

I'm convinced that every industry has a lighter, fun side to it. Perhaps you have to dig a bit to really find it, but it's there. Below is a chart of examples for five industries with just a few topic ideas for each.

Industry	Ideal Client	Topics of Entertainment
Real Estate	First time buyer	Local parks, gardening, cooking, decorating, coupons, eateries
Chiropractic	Mother in mid 30s	Fun & healthy food menus, yoga, spiritual, books, healthy places to eat
Beauty/Fashion	Women ages 20-30	New hairstyles, clothing, celebrity news, colors, budget friendly places to shop
Fitness/Sports	Men ages 25-40	Local bike trails, sports scores, golf, sports news, healthy eateries, nutrition news/trends
Restaurants (mid level)	Families and couples	Fun food photos, recipes, food trivia, food quotes, kid videos, animal videos

Social topics that relate to the mass population

In this area, we consider topics that have wide appeal and are popular. The way to evaluate whether or not a topic would fall into this category is to ask "Who would this affect, inform or entertain?" If you come up with multiple audience types, then you are on the right track. Here are just a few examples:

- News
- Trivia
- Travel
- Humor
- Quotes

You see how with just a few topics, you could enrich your social media presence and give your audience what they want – entertainment. Content for these areas is vast and easy to find on the Internet.

Events and subjects that everyone relates to

This is a smaller category, but a useful one in rounding out your content. Suggestions are:

- Holidays and key dates, such as an election or daylight savings time
- Local events and news
- Local sports team news

By putting the "social" in social media, you will achieve two things:

1. Increase the number of followers because you are giving them what they like
2. Show your customers and potential customers that you "get" them and can relate to them by showing your "social" side

Company/Business Promotion

But of course, your bottom line is to get more paying customers! And I'm sure you have A LOT to share that demonstrates how awesome your company is. There is absolutely room in social media for this! You *can and should* tell the world what you are all about. So where do you start?

Begin by thinking about your brand.

If you're a small business or a consultant, this may be a bit tricky. Do you have a company name? A logo? A tagline? Even if you don't, you should consider getting these. Once you have all these, social media can really highlight and brighten up your business identity – or brand.

Once you identify your brand, or if you already have a strong brand, then you can think of ways to promote it on social media. Photos are key! Photos of you, your logo, your business location, products and employees – you get the idea. With every aspect of company promotion, always keep your brand in mind.

What do you want to promote?

Ask yourself what you wish to accomplish with your promotions. Perhaps you are a restaurant with a new menu item. Perhaps you are a realtor with a hot new property to showcase. This content area will most likely change regularly.

Here are some generic company/business promotion ideas:

- New products
- Services
- Company history
- FAQs (Frequently asked questions) about your business
- Location information
- Employee of the month
- Highlights of a customer
- Promotions, coupons, deals and specials
- Jobs
- Photos and videos
- Customer testimonials

Depending upon your business, this social area can be interesting and informative. As long as you balance out your content with the additional content categories, you should have a rich social content strategy.

Before you continue with this book, take some time to come up with ideas in each category for your own business. This will help you craft content you can use while you go through the remaining chapters. In many ways, you are taking the items you wrote down on the last worksheet and delving deeper or answering the questions. Use the worksheet on the next page to help you organize your ideas.

* Social Media facts provided by www.thesocialskinny.com

Wordflirt Worksheet #2
Ideas for Creating Balanced Content

In each of the categories, create a list of topic ideas specifically for your target audience in relation to your industry and business. Some idea prompts are:

What can I teach my customers?
What questions can I answer?
What do my customers do in their free time?
What subjects are generic enough to interest my target audience?
What do I want to tell them about my company?

Educational Topics

_____

_____

_____

_____

_____

Entertainment Topics

_____

_____

_____

_____

Company/Business Information

_____

_____

_____

_____

_____

Chapter 4
Types of Content

✓ **FACT:** 93% of US adult Internet users are on Facebook
✓ **FACT:** The largest age demographic for Twitter Is 18-29, which represents 29% of the user base
✓ **FACT:** 4 out of 5 Internet users visit social networks and blogs*

Now that you've created your strategy for crafting great content, how are you going to deliver it? Again with your target audience in mind, you want to deliver your content in a variety of ways in order to keep them engaged. With the exception of Twitter, just writing a few sentences will work sometimes, but can get boring quickly for your audience.

There are many options available regarding how you deliver the messages you wish to convey. Below is a list of examples, some of which we will go into deeper in future chapters.

Top Three Types Of Content

Text – the traditional witty, smart or funny post that your audience will read on your Twitter feed, Facebook page, Google+ page or LinkedIn. At the very minimum, you should post text every day.

Photos – With the introduction of Pinterest and Instagram, photos have become extremely popular. As far as I know, you can add photos to every social media site that you have.

Videos – Videos are also popular and give your social media and your website added SEO advantages.

Additional Popular Content Types

The following list is of additional types of content that can be shared, although not every social media site accepts each type.

Contests
Contests are a fun way to engage your audience and can also be used as a tool for business.

Surveys
Surveys are also fun and encourage engagement. They could also result in valuable research information that you've now obtained from your customers or potential customers.

Deals or Coupons
You can offer special "Facebook Only" or "Twitter Only" types of deals to your customers.

Links to other articles

It is fairly common to share an article link and add a little description on the posting. If you are short on time and wish to get something posted quickly without a lot of thought, finding an article relevant to your industry and sharing the link is the way to go.

Links to other sites

Here is another easy way to post content quickly. You can find an appropriate website that you think your audience will like, write a description to post and then post the link.

Not as common

The following are possible, but not as common or popular for sharing on social media. For that reason, this book will not go into detail about them.

Audio Files – Not as popular or common as videos, but these can be uploaded to some of the social media sites. This is a great choice if you are a singer or a speaker and wish to showcase your voice. But it can also be used for an audio presentation or audio article.

Podcasts

If you've recorded a podcast and wish to offer it for free on your social sites, it is possible to upload it.

Webinar Recordings

Like podcasts, if you've recorded a webinar/presentation, you can upload this for viewing on your pages.

As the social media scene continues to evolve, there will likely be many more ideas that gain popularity. In the meantime, if you stick to the top three and sprinkle in some additional topics, you will have robust social media content!

* Social Media facts provided by www.thesocialskinny.com

Chapter Five
Written Content That Sparkles

✓ **FACT:** 87% of small to mid-sized businesses say that social media has helped them either somewhat or a great deal in the past year.

✓ **FACT:** More than 80% of small to mid-sized businesses plan to increase their use of social media in 2013

✓ **FACT:** 92% of US companies now use social media in their marketing efforts*

Knowing that you have more than one type of content to share with your audience can be overwhelming, so let's look first at written content. Written content was one of the first content types to hit the scene and continues to be a key ingredient to a solid social media strategy. Even on the photo and video sharing sites, you will need to add searchable written content in the form of descriptions or highlight about your post.

I'm going to break it down for you, beginning with where we left off at the end of Chapter 3.

You Are the Expert

No matter what industry you are in, you are the expert of your business domain! Whether you own a restaurant, retail operation, consulting business, car dealership, real estate office, medical practice or any other profession, you have knowledge about your industry and business that your audience needs to know. If you take some time to craft written content that represents your knowledge, you will be viewed as the expert in your field.

So you have all of this information in your head and you need to get it down on virtual paper. Let's break it down into three steps:

1. Break Down Areas of Interest

Take the list you created which represents your target audience's areas of interest. Break it down further into micro-topics under each topic. For example, using our list for a pet store owner, we'll take the first item on the list: *"Tips on how to care for your animal"*.

You could break this topic down into micro-topics such as the following:

- Grooming
- Diet
- Exercise
- Veterinary
- Love and attention

You could then break it down further and have these categories for each type of pet that your store supports, such as dogs, cats, fish, birds and reptiles. Your one area of interest has now become ten! Do this for each area of interest before moving to the next step. Use the worksheet at the end of the chapter for guidance.

2. Brainstorm

Pretend you are talking to a customer who doesn't know anything about your industry, but they are interested and want to know more. How would you begin? Topic by topic, brainstorm questions that your customer might have that you can answer. For a first time home buyer, I've brainstormed fifteen questions they might have:

- What credit rating do I need to have to get a home loan?
- How do I get a home loan?
- When do I get a home loan?
- Can I get pre-approved for a home loan?
- How can I improve my credit rating?
- What neighborhoods would be a good fit for me?
- What are the schools like in my target neighborhood?
- What is a home inspection?
- Do I need a home inspection?
- How much can I expect to pay in closing costs?
- What is escrow?
- How long is escrow?
- Can my deal fall through?
- What role will my realtor take?
- What are property taxes?

These are just a few questions – if you are a realtor focusing on first time homebuyers, you probably know many more questions that come up from your customer. Write all of these down. You may find that you add to the list in the days and weeks ahead and that's good! Once you have a solid list, you could print it out and post it where you can see it. This will serve as a foundation to your written posts. Use the worksheet at the end of the chapter to brainstorm.

3. Provide Answers

Now that you've identified the questions your target audience has, you simply need to write content that provides the answers. To begin, write as many paragraphs as you can for each answer. Don't worry about quality or making it sound like a how-to article – just get the information written. Use the worksheet at the end of the chapter for this exercise.

Fifteen Second Rule

The next step is to break down the answers into smaller chunks, which become your posting content. Consider that your audience will only spend about 15 seconds on your post, so keep it brief but informative. This probably means only a couple of sentences. Ta Da! You now have expert written content for your target audience!

Format for Twitter

Many of you are already avid tweeters or have at least heard of Twitter, which is considered a micro-blog. Here are a few quick tips on how to craft your content for Twitter:

Length: You only have 140 characters, so use them wisely! I'm not a big fan of using one letter to represent a word, such as r = are or u=you, but it's widely accepted as a way to shorten a word to make room to say more. You be the judge for yourself.

Let's break down how to write a Tweet by answering one of the questions in our example.

Q. What is a home inspection?

Tweet Answer:
A home inspection checks every aspect of your home before you buy.

Twitter has a character counter, so you can see how many characters you have left. In this case, there are 74 characters left. Now you might be wondering, why stop there? It's because you'll want to leave room for links, @mentions or hashtags.

What are Hashtags (#) and @ Mentions?

Hashtags: *Hashtags, or the # symbol, are used to make your tweets searchable.*

People look for others to follow that are tweeting about topics they have interest in. By putting a # (hashtag) in front of a key word, people will then find your tweet when they search your key word. Let's add this to our Tweet Answer:

A home inspection checks every aspect of your home before you buy #homebuyer

@Mention: *@ Mentions alert people that you have mentioned them in a tweet.*

For example, let's say that one of your followers asked the original question. We'll give him a twitter name of JohnDoe. By placing an @ in front of his twitter name, he and all of his followers now see your response. Let's also add this to our Tweet Answer:

@JohnDoe A home inspection checks every aspect of your home before you buy #homebuyer

Now you have a complete tweet that is searchable and others can see what an expert you are about home inspections.

Facebook, LinkedIn, Google+ & MySpace

Not all social media sites require you to limit your posts, but still, people do not have a long attention span when it comes to skimming over their social media sites. So whatever you say has to be clever, informative, relevant and showcase you as an expert…but not very long! On a positive note, you can now expand your brief answer into more information. Let's re-work our Tweet Answer and make it work for the other sites by giving it more context.

A home inspection will check every aspect of your home, from top to bottom, inside and out before you close escrow. It protects the buyer from any hidden, costly repairs and protects the seller from a future lawsuit. Every buyer should insist on a home inspection when buying a home.

I hope you can now see the difference between Twitter posts and what you can post on Facebook, LinkedIn, Google+ and MySpace.

Links

For every post where it makes sense, it's a good idea to provide a link to your website, blog, product information or whatever else you wish to sell. Twitter has a link "shrinker" that you can click on if your link is particularly long. Or you can sign up for a free bit.ly account and track how many clicks you receive on each of your links. Use the worksheet at the end of the chapter to format your topics into postable format.

Put It All Together

So far, you have:

- Created a list of "Areas of Interest"
- Broken the list down into a series of questions your customer would have
- Written answers in detail to all of the questions
- Broken down the answers into social media posts formatted for both Twitter and the other main Social sites.

What's next?

Congratulations! You now have relevant, expert content that you can begin sharing asap! In a later chapter, we will discuss automation, but for now, just start by posting some of your custom content posts and watch what happens. Consistency, coupled with your great content, is the key to increase your followers.

Next, we look at spicing up your social media content with photos.

* Social media facts provided by Tom Pick at www.busines2community.com

Wordflirt Worksheet #3
Creating Micro-Topics

Take your list from Worksheet #2 to create your micro-topics. Simply write the topics that could be broken down from your key areas of interest.

Educational Topic #1: _____
Micro-topics

_____

_____

_____

Educational Topic #2: _____
Micro-topics

_____

_____

_____

Educational Topic #3: _____
Micro-topics

_____

_____

_____

Entertainment Topic #1: _____
Micro-topics

_____

_____

_____

Entertainment Topic #2: _____
Micro-topics

_____

_____

Entertainment Topic #3: _____
Micro-topics

_____

_____

_____

Company/Business Topic #1: _____
Micro-topics

_____

_____

_____

Company/Business Topic #2: _____
Micro-topics

_____

_____

_____

Company/Business Topic #3: _____
Micro-topics

_____

_____

_____

Additional Topics: _____
Micro-topics

_____

_____

_____

Additional Topics: _____
Micro-topics

_____

_____

_____

Wordflirt Worksheet #4
Brainstorm Questions Your Target Audience has

Questions come from a need or desire for more information. Your job is to determine which questions your target audience has for which YOU can provide answers. Many of the questions begin as follows:

How do I…?
Where can I find more information about…?
What do I do if…?

Your list of questions for your target audience:

_____

_____

_____

_____

_____

_____

_____

_____

_____

_____

_____

_____

_____

_____

Wordflirt Worksheet #5
Providing Answers to the Questions From Your Target Audience

Write a paragraph answer for each of the questions that you listed on Worksheet #4. You are only providing information at this point – don't worry about making it pretty.

Answer to Question #1

_____

_____

_____

_____

_____

Answer to Question #2

_____

_____

_____

_____

Answer to Question #3

_____

_____

_____

_____

Answer to Question #4

_____

_____

Answer to Question #5

_____

_____

_____

_____

Answer to Question #6

_____

_____

_____

Answer to Question #7

_____

_____

_____

_____

Additional Answers and Notes

_____

_____

_____

_____

_____

Wordflirt Worksheet #6
Formatting Your Posts

Take your answers from the previous worksheet and put them in the right format for Twitter (140 characters or less) and Facebook, LinkedIn and Google+.

Formatted Answer to Question #1

Twitter:

_____

_____

FB/LI/G+:_____

_____

_____

_____

Formatted Answer to Question #2

Twitter:

_____

_____

FB/LI/G+:_____

_____

_____

_____

Formatted Answer to Question #3

Twitter:

_____

_____

_____

FB/LI/G+:_____

_____

_____

_____

Formatted Answer to Question #4

Twitter:

_____

_____

FB/LI/G+:_____

_____

_____

_____

Formatted Answer to Question #5

Twitter:

_____

_____

FB/LI/G+:_____

_____

_____

_____

Formatted Answer to Question #6

Twitter:

_____

_____

FB/LI/G+:_____

_____

_____

Formatted Answer to Question #7

Twitter:

_____

_____

FB/LI/G+:_____

_____

_____

More Answers...

Twitter:

_____

_____

FB/LI/G+:_____

_____

_____

_____

Twitter:

_____

_____

FB/LI/G+:_____

_____

_____

_____

Chapter 6
Using Photos to Spice Up Your Social Media

✓ **FACT:** As much as 70% of all likes, comments and shares in Facebook are related to photographs
✓ **FACT:** Pinterest grew faster than any other website in history in less than 1 year
✓ **FACT:** Instagram drives more traffic (links to websites) than Google+, LinkedIn and YouTube combined! Additionally, it receives more than 575 million "likes" per SECOND!*

What was the first thing that caught your eye on this page? Was it the words or the images of the photos? Often times our eyes gravitate toward images before text, especially if you are more visually oriented. So integrating images into your social media campaign will attract more interest and appeal to a wider audience.

In fact, the facts on the previous page represent important data regarding the power of images/photos. Instagram and Pinterest are photo-sharing social media sites. Many people are visual, by nature, and with the availability of quality photos on the many mobile devices, they can take and view pictures right in their hands wherever they go.

Pinterest and Instagram are not the only photo-sharing social media sites, but they are the leaders at the moment. You can (and should!) also post photos directly on all the other social media sites, including Twitter.

So how do you spice up your social media content with photos? First, you have to revert back to your target audience to consider what they might be interested in. Similar to written content, consider what gives your follower value and also showcases your expertise.

Products

If your business has products to sell, then sharing images of these products is a no-brainer! You not only can take photos of the products themselves, but also perhaps of customers using the products. If your product is intimate in nature, of course you would not want to do this! However, you could provide photos of what the product represents.

Let's use the pet store as our example. Here are six ideas for photos to share:

1. New pet arrivals in all categories

2. Pet food products
3. Customers with their pets
4. Pet "bling"
5. The store or sections of the store
6. Your team of employees with products

If you're a realtor, your products are the properties for sale or a property you just found for your buyer. If you are an auto dealership, you already know how important photos are for your business. If you own a restaurant, bakery, coffee shop or ice cream parlor – photos of your food and patrons enjoying your food would be perfect! Be sure to check out the chapter on 201 Ideas for Social Media Content for more inspiration.

Services

A service-based business can take a bit more creativity to showcase in photos, but certainly can be done! What if you're a mortgage broker or a banker? What if you are a life coach or a fitness expert? What if you wash windows or are a handyman? Or you are a nanny, gardener, teacher, medical practitioner or a dentist? You might be asking how you can *show* what you do in pictures. Here are five ideas of photos to share for a service business:

1. You, your team and/or your place of business
2. Before and after photos of your service
3. Tools used in your business, such as a hammer, exercise equipment, calculator, lawnmower, etc.
4. Cartoons or graphic images of you performing your service
5. Images of what your service represents, such as money, good health, love, family, children, happiness, nature, etc.

Get creative about how you can use images to post on social media that represents your service.

Your Industry

Now that you have ideas for promoting your business, consider the ways in which you can enrich your follower based on their needs as defined in Chapter 2. How can you apply their interests and needs to photos?

Adapting your written content

One way to put images into your social media is to add a photo to your written content posts. For example, say you are the realtor focused on first time buyers. Let's take the sample Tweet and Facebook post about home inspections and add an image. You can attach a photo such as the one below.

Now you have an image that represents the information in your post.

Words can also be turned into images and are quite popular, based upon what I see in my news feed on Facebook! Quotes, sentences, or simply power words, can be made to look nice with a bit of editing of the font and then made into a photo. You can buy them, link to them or make them yourself. Here is an example:

If you can find or make images that relate to your business, this is ideal. But sometimes just sharing a quote or message is good to do.

Where to Find Images

You don't have to hire a professional photographer or be one to get images into your social media campaigns. Taking your own photos of your team, products, services, customers and/or locations can be done with just about any smartphone these days and you can instantly upload it into social media.

In addition to creating your own images, you can "tag" or re-share photos from your audience's news feed or tweets. Be sure to give them credit when you do. On Instagram and Pinterest, you find things on the Internet to share or share your own.

The third way to add photos to your content, is to purchase royalty free photos. There are a number of royalty free photo sites, including www.bigstockphoto.com and www.istockphoto.com. You can purchase a single photo or buy packages of credits. You should read the terms of agreement and then you are able to use the photos you purchase on your blog, social media sites and/or other physical marketing material.

Infographics

Recently, Infographics have gained popularity on social media. An Infographic is an image that relates information by mixing graphics and information to make it appealing and easy to read. It is a good way to combine marketing and sales into an image that you can publish on your blog or on your social sites. See the example below for an example. I created this simple Infographic for Social Recruiting, but you don't have to create your own. There are many Infographics available online that you can simply share or you can purchase one from one of the royalty free photo sites mentioned previously.

Summary

Now that you see the value and ease of adding photos to spice up your social media, get organized! Create folders on your computer desktop and begin collecting photos to share. Then observe the level of engagement and interest in what you are posting to assess what your audience enjoys. Use the worksheet to help you identify images that you can share.

*Facts provided by thesocialskinny.com and prdaily.com

Wordflirt Worksheet #7
Ideas for Photos to Share on Social Media

Create a list of photos you already have or can get for your business.
Break them down into the following categories:

Photos of My Company Products

_____

_____

_____

_____

_____

_____

Service Related Photos (can purchase these, if needed)

_____

_____

_____

_____

_____

Industry Related Photos (can purchase these, if needed)

_____

_____

_____

_____

_____

Infographics (Google these or find them on royalty free sites)

Chapter Seven
Video: The Secret Sauce

- ✓ **FACT:** Video results appear in about 70% of the top 100 listings, the type of content most often displayed in universal or blended search results
- ✓ **FACT:** Online video was the fastest growing ad format in 2012 with nearly 55% growth
- ✓ **FACT:** Visitors who view product videos are 85% more likely to buy than visitors who do not*

If photos add spice to your social media campaigns, then using video is the *ultimate secret sauce*! Video is a fantastic way to show your audience and potential customers, not only who you are and what you're offering, but it begins creating a relationship the moment they view the video!

A big misconception that many business owners have, is that they have to appear in front of a camera to make a video for their company. That is not true! There are many options, both inexpensive and higher priced, that will help you "go Hollywood" without being in front of a video camera.

Before we explore those options, however, let's say you WANT to be in your own video. Where do you start? Here are six simple steps that you can follow.

Six Steps to Creating a Video

1. Define Your Objective

What do you hope to achieve with this video? Are you trying to drive traffic to your site? Do you want to introduce yourself and your business? Do you have a special offer? Become clear on your expected outcome before you proceed to the next step.

2. Define Your Topic

Next, go back to your list of topics to decide what your topic will be. If your topic is broad, then you may need to break it up into sub-topics. Your video should be between 1-4 minutes to ensure viewers watch the whole thing. Make a list of the topics you'd like to cover and pick the one with which you would like to start.

3. Write a Script

Maybe you are GREAT when thinking on your feet and can improvise your video to perfection in one take. Or maybe you are like the rest of the world and can't! Write a script that feels right to you and read it out loud to make sure it flows properly. Read it several times before you try to film yourself. While you do want to appear natural, you also want it to flow smoothly.

4. **Record Your Video**
   You don't have to have expensive equipment to record a quality video. Most smartphones allow you to take video, upload it to your computer and edit it. You can ask a friend or colleague to hold the camera while you speak or if you have a camcorder with a tripod, you can do it yourself.

   When you record your video, I recommend that you don't stop the camera. If you mess up, just start again. You can edit out the mistakes later. Do this until you are satisfied that you have enough recorded to complete your video. Or if you must stop, you don't have to start all over. You can put the clips together and edit them by keeping the good parts.

5. **Edit Your Video**
   There are many video editing software programs available today, if you would like to edit your video yourself. If you already know how to do this, then great – go for it.

   If you do not know how to edit video, then consider outsourcing this part of the process. If your video is short and you have little to no budget, you could find someone on **www.fiverr.com** to edit it for you. Fiverr is a site where people will perform certain tasks for only $5 USD. Using Fiverr is hit or miss sometimes, so you may be better off hiring someone from **www.elance.com** or **www.freelancer.com**. These sites have very high quality freelancers from around the world. They bid on your project and you pick the contractor to complete the work. All work is done through their website to monitor quality and deadlines.

6. **Upload Your Video**
   Once you are happy with your video, create a YouTube channel for your business and upload your video. YouTube is the most popular video sharing, social media site and is powered by Google. This means that your video has more gusto when it comes to showing up on search engines, such as Google. You should also upload the video to other video sites (VIMEO, etc), Facebook, Google+, your blog, LinkedIn and wherever else

you can. Be sure to include links to your website in each upload description!

Interviews

If you know of people in your field that are experts on particular topics, ask them for an interview. If they agree to the interview, be sure to give them the topic questions ahead of time so that they can prepare their thoughts. Make sure to give them credit and provide links to their website.

Video Tour

If you own a business establishment where customers visit, consider a video tour of your facility. If you have a kitchen or production area, take them on a tour of it as if they were your guest and you were showing them around. This kind of "behind the scenes" look at your business can be fun and entertaining as well.

Screencasts

If you are **not** interested in appearing in front of the camera, another great option is to film a screencast video. A screencast video uses software and a microphone to record whatever is on your computer screen. There are three things you can do with a screencast video:

1. You can demonstrate a product on your computer while recording it.
2. Use presentation software, such as PowerPoint or KeyNote to record your presentation as if you were live.
3. Create a slideshow and narrate it.

Let's take a look at each option more closely.

Video Demonstration

If you have an Internet-based product, software or a website to sell, a video demonstration is a great way to educate your customers and drive traffic to your website and business. Camtasia is a great screencasting software, with full editing capability. The steps to creating a video demo from your computer are:

1. Determine what you want to demonstrate – you will want to make sure to include all the major features and their BENEFITS. If there are too many for a short video, break it up into the major features/benefits for more videos.
2. Write a script and practice it prior to recording
3. Record your demo using screencast software such as Camtasia.

4. Edit out the parts you don't like or hire an editor on a freelance website
5. Post to YouTube and Vimeo
6. Post to your website

Presentation Video

Have you done a presentation for your business that you can share through video? If you've already prepared and delivered one, then this should be easy. Simply record the slideshow using the script you used for your presentation, edit and post.

If you don't already have a prepared presentation, then you can prepare one for recording. Here are some ideas for topics:

- How-To -Train viewers on a particular topic that you have knowledge of that relates to your business. For example, if we use the pet store example, you could prepare a presentation about "Steps to cleaning a fish bowl" or "Tools you need to groom a dog". It doesn't have to be long – in fact, shorter is better.
- Facts and Information – Maybe your goal is to create awareness of your product or industry. Researching and presenting facts related to your topic can be delivered via a presentation video.
- Answer a Question – LinkedIn is a great place to find people in groups who are discussing your favorite topics. Look around for questions that are being asked for which you know the answer. Create a short presentation video that answers the question.

Video Scribe

In the last few years, video scribe (also called whiteboard animation) has become popular. This option is somewhat expensive but the popularity and conversion rates of viewers are huge!

A good video scribe company will help you to come up with a script and then animate the video for you. They are the experts in how to "tell a story" about your topic. This option is very good for sales videos.

Photo Slide Shows

You can also put together a slideshow of your products, team and/or your business in action. This can make a great 60 second video without using your presence or your voice on camera. And most likely, you have a good collection of images already.

Final Thoughts On Video

Video in social media is going to continue to gain ground in popularity with it's wide appeal and the ease for which videos can now be shared. In my experience, there are a few things to keep in mind:

1. Keep it short – people do not have a very good attention span these days so a video that is less than two minutes will probably be more successful for you than one which is five minutes long.
2. Organic is good – don't over-produce your video to make it slick and perfect. Professional, yes, but not too professional or it will look like a commercial on TV.
3. Consider a series – if your presentation video is too long, chunk it down into a series of two minute videos by separating the topics into small pieces. This will give you much more exposure and traffic!

* Factual data from emarketer, Marketing Week and Internet Retailer

Wordflirt Worksheet #8
Plotting Out Your Video Ideas

List your ideas for each type of video. You don't need to write a script yet, just brainstorm on the various ways you could showcase your business in video format.

Interviews with Experts or Colleagues in My Industry

_____

_____

_____

_____

Video Tours or Computer Screencasts

_____

_____

_____

_____

Presentation video (could be a "how-to" or sales video)

_____

_____

_____

_____

Photo Montage or Slideshow

_____

_____

_____

_____

Chapter 8
Contests, Surveys and Deals, Oh My!

✓ **FACT:** Photo or video contests result in more engagement than simple sweepstakes
✓ **FACT:** 70% of users want a rewards program from brands they follow
✓ **FACT:** 67% of customers will like a Facebook page to save 25% or more*

Providing great content is not just about pushing information out to your audience. It's about engaging them and encouraging participation. You want your audience to have fun with your social media sites or gain value by getting deals. This chapter focuses on engaging content such as contests, surveys and deals.

Contests

You don't have to have your own company product to award in order to have a contest. Any business at all can conduct a contest. You'd be amazed at the people that respond to a contest even if the prize is a $10 gift card!

Here are some guidelines for hosting a contest on social media:

- Determine your objective – what are you trying to accomplish? Do you want more followers (or "Likes")? Do you want your followers to become customers? Do you want help creating user generated content (such as a photo contest)? Before you decide what and how to give a prize for a contest, determine your objective.
- Determine the Venue – which social media site would you like to use for the contest? Facebook is the best for this type of engagement, but I suppose you could have a contest on any of the social sites.
- What do you want them to do? Decide what the contest will be (ideas in the next section). Make sure you are completely clear about what entrants should do and how they should submit their entries.
- Who will be the judge? You could determine the winner based upon how many "likes" and shares they have. Or you could have your team decide. However you wish to judge the contest, write down the guidelines and make them available to the entrants.
- How long is the contest? Make sure you have plenty of time for people to enter, but not too much time that they lose interest. I find that 3-4 weeks is pretty good. Again, make these guidelines available to your entrants.
- Determine your prizes – if you don't have a lot of engagement already on your site, you should consider giving away a valuable prize such as an iPad or Kindle. This will make it worthwhile for the people that might be on the fence about participating. It should also be directly related to the amount of work one will have to do to enter the contest. If you just want more "likes" then that is easy for someone to do. If you're asking them to do a testimonial video, that is more creative and takes more time, so a larger prize would be better.

- Advertise – if you don't already have a pretty large following and your objective is to get more followers, then paid advertising would be a good option. You could advertise on other social media sites to drive traffic to the site where you are holding your contest. Don't forget to Tweet about it too! If you're a brick and mortar business, have flyers, table tents or just signs telling your customers about the contest.
- Announce the results – once your contest is complete, be sure to share the winner's name and their entry, if applicable. Feature them on your blog or just in your social media posts. And above all, deliver the prize as promised in your guidelines!

Resources

In order to run a successful contest on Facebook, you may need to use a third party app. **www.appbistro.com** has a variety of apps and many of them are free.

Contest Ideas

Photo contests – your products, people using your products

Name it – name a new product or service

Tagline – determine a tagline for a product or service

Video contests – using the products or a testimonial video

Recipe contest – People love to share recipes and to get new recipes.

For additional contest ideas, see the chapter on 101 content ideas

Surveys

Another feature available to help you interact with your audience or to gain new followers, is the survey feature. While there is a statistical science behind true data gathering, using surveys in social media doesn't have to be complicated or require a doctorate to conduct. Sometimes simple is better and just asking 3-5 questions can achieve the results you want.

You can do many things with surveys, so really get creative! Here are a few ideas:

Preferences – If you're not sure what your customers want, using a survey is a fantastic way to find out!

Menu Items – If you're a restaurant and you're considering a menu makeover, this is a great way to figure out how to structure your new menu.

Product – Ask your audience what to name a new product or give them a choice of products and ask them which one they are more likely to buy.

Knowledge base – Want to know how much your audience knows on a particular topic? Ask them to rate their knowledge on a scale of 1-5 for each aspect of the topic.

Customer Satisfaction – This one is a very helpful tool if you're looking for feedback and is critical to improving your business over the long term.

Demographics – Want to know who your ideal client is? By taking a demographic poll, you can find out the age, gender, race and other demographic information that can help you with your marketing.

Market Research – In general, you can conduct any type of market research by using a survey or poll.

A few words of advice about surveys and polls:

- There is no need to reinvent the wheel. Sites such as Survey Monkey offer certified templates to help you get started.
- If you're looking for new followers, you can use paid advertising to invite people to take your survey.
- Most online survey sites have a FREE version, which may be a good place to start. However, if you already have a lot of followers that you feel would engage with you, then you may wish to pay for the mid-level survey product.

Deals

83% of customers are looking for a deal or a coupon on social media. Coupons and Deals are a huge way to acquire new customers or to increase business with current customers.

If you have ever had a hard copy coupon promotion or discount, then this should be familiar to you with a slight twist: you are sharing a deal on social media instead of print or your website.

Retail

For businesses that sell products, *what* you offer should be fairly straightforward. Here are several ideas:

- Buy One Get One Free – this is hugely popular these days as even the big retailers have these types of specials.
- 10% - 50% off discounts.
- Product of the day – consider choosing a product each day, week or month that you feature as a deal.
- First customers to order – you give away something to the first 50 customers that others would usually have to pay for
- Group coupons – sites such as Groupon and LivingSocial offer "bulk" deals where your customers share the deal they got and if so many of their friends buy it, they get it for free.
- Give away – if your customer buys one product, you throw in something for free. This is a good way to get customers to try a new product that you'd like to promote that they might not otherwise buy.

Restaurants

Like retail, if you own a restaurant, bakery, deli or coffee shop, your offer should be pretty easy to determine. Here are several ideas:

- $1, $2 or $5 off the entire order
- 10% - 50% discount on their order
- Buy One Get One Free – this could be a meal, coffee drink, bakery item or sandwich
- Daily Special – is Tuesday Salad day? Maybe Friday Happy Hour? Offer something free for specific days of the week
- Clearance – if you have product left at the end of the day, consider posting or tweeting that you are having a clearance special. You could say something like "Today from 3 pm until

closing, when you buy a cupcake, you get two free!" This will drive traffic to your restaurant on an otherwise slow day.

Services

If you don't have products, but rather, you provide a service there are also deals that you could offer. Here are some ideas:

- 10% - 50% off the cost of the service.
- Free movie tickets when a client places an order (or something free that resonates with your business).
- Referral discount – if your client refers a new client to you, offer them a discount or a free service.
- Throw in something for free – if your business has a menu of services that you offer, you could throw in something when the client orders. Examples include: "We'll clean ten windows in your home for free when you book two home cleaning appointments" or "we'll draft your power of attorney when you purchase an estate plan from us" or "we'll give you a teeth whitening kit for new dental patients". It doesn't have to be a big give away, but certainly something that will be attractive enough to bring customers in.
- Book giveaway – if you've written a book on your expertise or you know of one that is good for your clients, give them a copy.

Summary

When it comes to contests, surveys and deals, there are tons of things you could do, depending upon your industry. Get creative and have fun with it. Add a slice of humor and personal touch to all you do and you will get the engagement (and business!) you're looking for.

*Social Media facts provided by **www.thesocialskinny.com** and emarketer.

Wordflirt Worksheet #9
Ideas for Contests, Surveys and Deals

What engagement activities can you think of to increase your following and your business? Write them in the space below.

Contest Ideas

_____

_____

_____

_____

_____

_____

Survey Questions

_____

_____

_____

_____

_____

Coupons or Deals to offer (include any limits or exclusions)

_____

_____

_____

_____

_____

Chapter 9
Blogging Juice for Your Business

- ✓ **FACT:** 57% of companies say they generated sales through their blogs
- ✓ **FACT:** Companies that publish 15 or more blog articles per month generate FIVE times more web traffic than companies that don't blog.
- ✓ **FACT:** There are now 70 million Wordpress blogs and 39 million Tumblr blogs worldwide!*

If you're not sure exactly what a blog is, I can guarantee that if you've spent any time on the Internet at all, then you've probably read a blog or many blogs! Blogs are simply articles that one writes on their website. It could be an informational article, a fun loving article or a rant. It is a place for people to write about their passion, their business, their family, their journeys.

I've heard a lot of buzz about blogging...that it's overdone. What's the point? That it's soooo last year! I don't agree.

In fact, I feel blogging is important for four reasons:

1. You get to showcase yourself as an expert, no matter what industry you are in
2. You round out your community of customers and potential customers by providing them with valuable and relevant information that expands upon your social media sharing
3. You build trust and loyalty when you use this as a form of content marketing
4. By blogging, you are creating a dynamic website that Google will love and will get you higher ranking on the search engine results when people Google your key words.

How To Create a Blog

This is not a technical book about how to design a blog site. However, there are free and easy tools out there that you can use to create your own blog. Google's free site is **www.blogger.com** and a very popular free blogging site is **www.wordpress.com**. If you already have a website, you can simply add a tab to your menu and create a page whereby you can write articles whenever you wish.

If all of this is overwhelming to you, then consider hiring someone to set it up for you.

Create a Plan

Similar to the way that you created your social media production schedule, you should take some time to plan out your blogging topics and a schedule.

Before you begin, ask yourself the following questions:

1. How often can you (or one of your team members) realistically write a blog article?
2. Whom do you wish to reach?
3. What do you wish to communicate?
4. What does your target audience wish to know or hear about from you?

Create a List

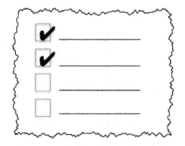

Once you've answered these questions, brainstorm on article ideas. Hint: use the list you created for social media to come up with ideas that you can expand into a 400-600 word article. Brainstorm on as many ideas as you can during this phase. You can always add or remove ideas as you go.

Break up your ideas into common topics. For example, if you are an Insurance Agent, you could break the topics up the following ways:

- Home Insurance

- Auto Insurance
- Health Insurance
- Life Insurance
- Disability Insurance
- Long Term Care Insurance

Depending, of course, on which areas are your specialty.

A word of caution: when you are writing your list of topics, steer away from those which are self-serving. If you only write about your business and how awesome you are, your readers will not stay on your site long, nor will they be back. Consider what your reader wants to know about, not what you want them to know about you.

Create a Schedule

Since you asked yourself how often you can realistically write, plot out the dates on the calendar and assign blog post topics to each entry. If you're worried about not getting around to it, also block out a couple of hours on your actual calendar that you will dedicate to writing your blog posts.

Writing Blitz

I find it helpful to block out a few hours each month to write 3 or 4 blog articles that I will use during that month. If I can write more, great! But tackling several articles at one sitting checks it off the list until the next month.

Be sure to include your key words in your article titles so that you can rank higher in the search engines (SEO). Also, by naturally using your key words throughout your blog post, you will rank higher.

Share!

Now that you have a blog set up and you've begun writing, be sure to share it! Even though you will get organic traffic to your blog post when people run a search on your key words, you still want to get it out to your audience. Post a link on all of your social media sites. Tweet about it and schedule additional tweets for the rest of the week. If you belong to any groups on LinkedIn or Facebook, be sure to post a link to your article there as well.

Put sharing options on the actual blog so that others can share it too. You can also set up an RSS feed whereby others can sign up to receive notification automatically whenever you write a new post.

Additional Tips

Back it up - Make sure you have a back up of not only your blog, but also your writing. Websites can go down and at times you could lose some of your work. Be sure to write your blog posts in another program, such as Microsoft Word and keep a copy on your computer. That way, if you do have to recover your blog, you have all of your articles to recreate it.

Include images in your posts - Images capture the essence of what you are writing by providing a visual enhancement to your words. (And your viewers can PIN it!)

Use Video – if you enjoy being in front of the camera, consider using a video for your blog (called a Vlog). You can speak into the camera as if you are teaching a short segment of a class. This gives you additional content to share on YouTube and gives your audience more of YOU.

* Facts provided by **www.business2community.com** and **www.thesocialskinny.com**

Wordflirt Worksheet #10
Planning Your Blog Content

Answer the following questions to determine how much blogging you can realistically do.

How often can you (or one of your team members) realistically write a blog article?

_____

_____

_____

Whom do you wish to reach?

_____

_____

_____

What do *you* wish to communicate?

_____

_____

_____

_____

What does your target audience wish to know or hear about from you?

_____

_____

_____

_____

_____

Wordflirt Worksheet #11
Your List of Blog Article Ideas

Using your list of topics from Chapter 5, expand those subjects into potential 400-600 word blog posts. Either list the subjects, or possible headlines.

_____

_____

_____

_____

_____

_____

_____

_____

_____

_____

_____

_____

_____

_____

_____

_____

_____

_____

_____

_____

_____

Wordflirt Worksheet #12
Your Blogging Schedule

Plot out a schedule of topics you will post on the days in which you will post them. There is a printable version of this worksheet at our website www.socialmediacontentforbusiness.com.

Week 1				
Monday	Tuesday	Wednesday	Thursday	Friday
Week 2				
Monday	Tuesday	Wednesday	Thursday	Friday
Week 3				
Monday	Tuesday	Wednesday	Thursday	Friday
Week 4				
Monday	Tuesday	Wednesday	Thursday	Friday

Chapter 10
Content Detective

✓ **FACT:** Facebook grew 18% in 2012 and represented more than half of all social content sharing
✓ **FACT:** LinkedIn gets the highest vote for driving B2B sales
✓ **FACT:** Moms are the largest demographic in America for using Pinterest at 61%*

Now that you know your target audience and have created a content strategy, you may be wondering how you are going to come up with all of the content for your Social Media. Luckily, you don't have to create it all yourself and there are plenty of resources available to help you!

Internet Research

I feel the very best tool available for finding social media content, is the Internet. You can pretty much find anything and everything you need for YEARS of social media content, but it will take a little research to get started. No matter what industry you are in, there are plenty of experts out there writing articles and blog posts.

Some tools that make this step quick and easy include:

Google Alerts – you can set up Google to send you an alert every time someone publishes something that uses the key words that you wish to follow.

Google Reader – You can also set up a Google Reader account where Google will automatically place information on your topic in your account so that you can go there to read what came up in searches. You get to configure these Google tools, so that you don't get too much information sent to you.

Compilation Websites – Sites such as Technorati or AllTop are aggregators of information in your industry. They offer a compilation of the latest news, blogs, posts, videos and other information that relates to the industry or topic you define.

So once you have identified articles or topics that interest you, how do you pull out the nuggets of information to create posts?

To get started, follow these steps:

1. Find topics that interest you using the aforementioned resources.
2. Read through the results until you find an article that provides you with information that you like.
3. Comb through the information, taking notes on the various aspects of the topic.
4. Write a tip or fact that you wish to share in your own words.
5. Format it for Twitter (140 characters or less) and an expanded version for Facebook, Google+ or LinkedIn.

6. Post it!

Let's do one together. We will use the pet store industry as our example.

1. The topic will be dog grooming, so the keyword we will use to search Google, is "dog grooming tips". Here is the first page of the results:

(Close up)

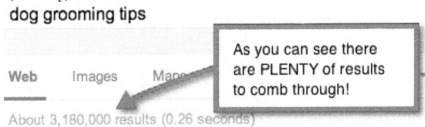

If you click on the first selection after the promotional ads, you'll see this from Martha Stewart's website:

Pet Grooming Tips

★ ★ ★ ★ ☆   Rate   🔲 Comments (4)

 1 of 11 ▶

Shampooing Your Pet

Follow these steps for a thorough washing. Shampoo should be specific for the animal you're washing and low-foaming so it rinses away easily and does not strip nutrients from coat.
Use washcloth to wet pets's face.

Use hose or pitcher to wet rest of pet with warm water.

Start shampooing at face and work your way to tail.

Let shampoo set for several minutes.

Use washcloth to rinse shampoo from

2. From this, you could create a post that looks something like this:

Twitter Format: When shampooing your dog, use a wet washcloth to wet and rinse your dog's face. #doggrooming

Facebook and others: When shampooing your dog, a wet washcloth can be used to first wet the face and then rinse shampoo from it. The rest of the body can be wet and rinsed with either a hose or pitcher.

The point is to pull nuggets out of articles that are useful to your audience. Be sure to either paraphrase into your own words, or give credit to your source (such as a reference or a link to their site).

Other Documentation

Now that you've learned how to pull content out of articles and blogs on the Internet, you can do the same things with the following material:

- Industry magazines
- Books in your industry or on the specific topic
- Seminar materials
- Pamphlets you pick up at conferences or from competitors
- Podcasts, webinars you attend

Your Competition

Check out what your competition is up to. I'm not saying to steal their work, but you can certainly get ideas and tips from them as well. If you use what they are posting but re-write it with your own twist, it is perfectly acceptable.

PLR = PRIVATE LABEL RIGHTS

Private Label Rights (PLR)

If you are looking for material that you can use for either your Social Media posting or your blog, then you should consider buying some Private Label Rights or PLR. PLR is work which you purchase to be able to use for your own purpose.

These days you can buy PLR articles, ebooks, audio, video, website templates, photos and more.

There are a lot of options for PLR so it can be difficult to decide where to spend your money. Additionally, there are some low quality PLR sites where you could waste money to buy content that, well, basically stinks!

Here are some tips for buying PLR:

- Do your research. Before you buy any PLR, run a Google Search for "PLR Reviews" and read the appropriate articles.
- Find Affiliate Marketing or Internet Marketing groups on LinkedIn Groups or Facebook and ASK around about where you can buy quality PLR.
- Most sites offer a refund if you are not happy. I recommend looking at the quality of the content as soon as you sign up so that you don't miss the refund window if the PLR is not good

Guest Writers

If you do well with Social Media content, but find it difficult to write fresh blog posts on a regular basis, consider asking another expert in your field to write a post or a series of posts that you could feature. Most people would do this for you for free because they would get free advertising of their own business.

You will need to provide the guidelines for your guest, including length, topics to choose from (or let them suggest and you decide), the tone you wish to capture and whom you are targeting. Being clear up front will help you both make it a pleasant and cooperative experience.

Make sure that you include a brief bio of your guest and a link to their website. In addition, you could offer to reciprocate the favor, if you'd like to get additional exposure for your business.

Sharing Links

Perhaps my least favorite, but highly popular technique, is link sharing. I'm sure you've seen it where people simply share a link to what other people wrote or a link to the person who did the sharing. While this is a valid way to get exposure and visibility to your social sites, it doesn't truly showcase you as an expert or thought leader in your industry. I would say use this no more than 30% of the time.

In this day of the Internet, just about everything you need to know is at your fingertips. It just takes a little creativity and research. Use the worksheet to brainstorm ideas for where to get your content.

* Facts provided by **www.business2community.com**

Wordflirt Worksheet #13
Ideas for Where to Get Content

Keywords to use for Google Alerts, AllTop or just a general Google search:

_____

_____

_____

_____

_____

Websites or articles that have information for your topics.

_____

_____

_____

_____

_____

Other documents that you have or can buy for your topics

_____

_____

_____

_____

_____

PLR material and websites that provide it

_____

_____

_____

_____

_____

_____

What your competition is doing that can help you

_____

_____

_____

_____

_____

_____

Guest writers for your blog

_____

_____

_____

_____

_____

Websites you can use as links to share with your audience

_____

_____

_____

_____

_____

Notes or ideas

_____

_____

_____

_____

_____

Chapter 11
The Social Media Lifesaver: Automation

Now that you have determined your target audience, come up with a great strategy and gathered your content, it's time to put it all together. But the idea of taking hours every month to post your topics on Social Media can be overwhelming. So why not automate it?

Social Media Automation Tools

There are a variety of tools available at a reasonable price and some of them are even free. A few popular tools are:

Hootsuite
SocialOomph
TweetDeck
Buffer

Hootsuite

This is a social media tool that can be accessed anywhere, from any computer, and from any cell phone, so you can tweet or post on the go.

Being the most popular of the Social Media automation tools, there are several pros and cons you have to consider:

Pros of using Hootsuite

- You can have different streams on the same page, so you don't have to click back and forth like you do on Twitter.
- You can add more than one Twitter account, Google +, Facebook, LinkedIn and other social media tools, so you can manage it all in one place.
- You can also include your Wordpress blog.
- There are three solutions available: free, pro, and enterprise options.
- A bookmarking tool is included, allowing you to easily index and manage pages right when you are cruising the Internet. This is called a "Hootlet"
- You get the 30 day history, so you can look at old feeds, and information transmission.
- The paid versions allow you to design custom reports that analyze how your social media was received.
- The paid versions also allow you to add a team member at no extra cost

Cons of using Hootsuite

- Mobility integration software is not exceptional. While it's convenient, there are still a few quirks that don't work as well as they should.
- With the free version, analytic tools are lacking.
- You must enter the URL when you want to tweet a link into an auto shorten box (it can't be added directly to the tweet)
- There is a delay when you wish to refresh streams.

SocialOomph

I've used both SocialOomph and Hootsuite. I think they both offer very solid options for free and paid subscriptions. However, the paid version of SocialOomph costs more than Hootsuite, so I primarily use Hootsuite now.

Pros of SocialOomph

- The free version works pretty well for very basic functions
- Like all automation tools, it is high in utility value and saves you time.
- It is easy to set up and use, so it makes your social media posting quick and easy.
- Automatically tweets, at the right interval, so you solve the issues of over-tweeting.
- You can add more than one social media account to the mix and you can "schedule" posts to tweet.
- You can set up automatic direct messages to new followers.
- You get notifications (new followers, the keywords visitors used to find you, etc).
- If you purchase the professional package, you get a very rich engine to run your social media – far more than Hootsuite

Cons of using SocialOomph

- It is not glamorous, and is rather dull in appearance.
- You have to set time limits for the tweets and retweets to be sent out at.
- You have to purchase a professional account to include blogs and get all the features you want.
- If you want more, and better, you have to pay for it. And, being a bit dated, it does fall back in line to other automation tool options.

Buffer

A third option with Social Media automation tools is Buffer. Like the others, there are good and bad points.

Pros of using Buffer

- You post videos and photos, and Buffer automatically shares them throughout the course of the day.
- You can link up to 12 social accounts, such as twitter, Facebook, and others quickly, and access them from anywhere.
- You get free detailed analytics on all posts. From the likes on Facebook, to the follows on twitter, you can see it all.
- You can add 2 staff members to tweet, edit, or do anything on your Buffer account.
- You can use extensions, and share on Chrome, Firefox, IE, and Safari, in a matter of seconds.
- Straight forward and easy to use

Cons of using Buffer

- You have to download software to your desktop (not used through the Internet).
- You have to purchase the full version to get full access to all apps.
- If you add to Buffer (rather than tweet now), you might forget to send something
- The limit of 12 social media accounts could cause it to be too limited to those that have a lot of accounts, such as a social media manager or a business with a lot of different streams

Tweetdeck

Finally, I almost thought about NOT including this option, because it is strictly a Twitter based tool. However, if Twitter is your main social media venue, then these pros and cons may be useful to you.

Pros of using TweetDeck

- Real time views & easy to use scheduling system.
- Good for official tweets and unofficial retweets.
- The desktop version allows you to schedule tweets, and add multiple accounts.
- With your own bit.ly account, you can track analytic information and can send longer tweets.
- With the chrome version, you do not have to download and can access directly from Chrome, and it is a little more user friendly.
- After linking to different accounts, status updates are posted to the main stream.
- It's easy to set up and use this app.

Cons of using Tweetdeck

- Since it is strictly a twitter based tool, you cannot use it for Facebook, Google+, LinkedIn, blogs or other social media sites.
- With the desktop version, you must download it, so you can't use it on the go.
- There are no direct analytics on the site and you have to use bit.ly to get your analytics

A Reminder about Engagement

While it is easy to use these tools to "set it and forget it", I want to remind you that social media is all about engagement. Don't "forget it" to the point that you're not aware of how your followers are responding to you, your shares and your business as a whole. You must still keep an eye on your social media and respond to them. Otherwise you lose the point of using social media in the first place – which is to ENGAGE.

Summary

Automating your social media activities can make your life much easier. The tools that are available today are constantly evolving and new features are added all the time. Don't be afraid to try each of the tools to see which one works the best for you. You can always switch if you are not happy with the ease of use or the features of the one you start with.

(Note: Pros and Cons are based upon the offerings of each tool at the time this book was being written. Features and Updates may occur in the future and are not under the control of the author!)

Chapter 12
The Future of Social Media

As I finish up this book about social media content, I find myself wondering what new features, technology or trends could be in the future for Social Media. I never imagined that we would have this type of venue for networking and I can only wonder what else have I not imagined? Thank goodness for the technical geniuses that DO have the imagination to go where we have not been before. So what is next?

Questions I have are:

- Will it get easier to manage?
- Will one social media site take over all as a primary venue?
- Will mobile play a larger role?
- How much will content change?
- Will it even be called "Social Media" in a few years?

The truth of the matter is that Social Media is not a fad and it's not going away. Everyone from children to grandparents have embraced it, much the way people have embraced television or, more recently, the Internet.

I see that Social Media will continue to evolve and these are my predictions:

1. Mobile Usage Will Grow – It is estimated that by 2014, the number of mobile users will outnumber the actual number of people on the planet. WOW! Smartphones are now more accessible than ever and research shows that people are using their smartphones more than they use their computers.
2. Being on Social Media will be as important as having a website. – The way that everything mingles and links together and the ease of getting on Social Media will make it imperative that businesses have a social media presence.
3. Content will become more important – Even Google has changed it's algorithm on its searches to give higher ranking to websites with content that have high quality content. So, providing quality content, I predict, will not just be wanted, but will be demanded!
4. Companies will use it more for customer support – reputation management can easily get out of control when items on social media go viral. Companies will listen better and try to head off any major complaints.
5. Tools to measure Social Media will improve – Everyone keeps asking how you can measure your social media results and the answers are still vague and intangible. I predict that someone will invent a way to really nail down the analytics of a successful social media presence.
6. More Hacking on Social Media – You don't hear about it happening very often, but I think it will be more common that social media sites will get hacked. Companies like McAfee and Symantec should (or maybe they already are) work on solutions to this potential security issue.
7. Integration – I think a smart company will come along that integrates all of the social sites into one venue, so that you only

have to log on to one site in order to access, view and interact with all of your social media pages.

Summary

Whatever the future of Social Media, content will always be a crucial element. You are now armed with the means to have a robust social media strategy that will help your business succeed on Social Media.

Be sure to sign up for tips and tricks, new features and ideas and other social media content news at my website: http://www.wordflirtsocialmedia.com. My goal is to help you create GREAT social media content that keeps your customers interested and attracts new customers to your business. I also respond to inquiries if you email me at info@thewordflirt.com.

Enjoy the final chapter which I hope prompts you to get creative with your social media. Oh. And don't forget to like our page! www.facebook.com/thewordflirt

Until then – happy socializing!

201 Social Media Content Ideas for Business

Industry Related
1. News about your industry
2. Events happening for your industry
3. New laws for your industry
4. Products reviews
5. Services reviews
6. Opinions about things in your industry
7. Things that relate to your industry, but aren't your actual industry
8. Funny stories about your industry
9. Worthwhile quotes from experts in your industry
10. Facts and figures for your industry
11. How to tips for specific skills, actions, goals and results for your industry
12. Suggested reading for your industry
13. Additional resources for your industry

Causes
14. Facts about your cause
15. Resources to help people
16. Interviews with people that are victims of your cause
17. News about your cause
18. Breakthroughs associated with your cause
19. Success stories associated with your cause
20. Events related to your cause
21. Suggested reading for your cause
22. Website links for your cause

Your Product/Service Info
23. How to use your product (could be written or video)
24. Benefits of your product or service
25. Funny stories about your product or service
26. Testimonials from people using your product or service
27. Tips about your product or service
28. Meetups, seminars, webinars or other events associated with your product or service
29. Featured product of the month

Your Company info

30. Success stories related to your company
31. Employee of the month
32. Customer of the month
33. Job openings
34. Facts about your company
35. Neighborhood news
36. Neighborhood events
37. Charity or community service your company does
38. "Did you know…" about your company
39. Projects your company is working on
40. Early release teasers

Educational Seminars or Webinars (could be video and then post notifications on other social sites)

41. How-To Series with step by step instruction
42. Teach new techniques or changes in your industry
43. Discuss facts and historical data about your product, service or industry
44. Certifications
45. Teach how to sell your services or products

Coupons, discounts and deals

46. Buy one get one free
47. Percentage off of final sale
48. Percentage off of product of the month, day or week
49. Refer a friend and get something free
50. Refer a friend and both get something
51. Buy one package or product and get something free
52. "Like" us on Facebook and get something
53. Sign up early and get a discount
54. Mobile coupons (no need to have paper coupon)

Surveys

55. What's your favorite…?
56. Who do you think will win?
57. Compare products
58. Compare services
59. What would you like to see our company do better?

60. What new features, products or services would you like us to offer?
61. Customer service surveys
62. When do you think you would...buy, sell, trade-in, etc

Contests
63. Name the product
64. Photo contest related to your product or service
65. Video contest related to your product or service
66. Most creative testimonial video
67. Whoever gets the most likes or shares of something they post related to your product or service gets a prize
68. Recipe contest using your product
69. Funniest story related to your product, service or industry
70. Raise the most money for your cause and win something

Photos
71. Infographics for your industry (facts portrayed in a graphical format to make it easy to digest)
72. You, the business owner
73. Your employees
74. Your location (if brick and mortar)
75. Your products
76. Your customers
77. People using your products
78. Events you hold
79. Community service you or your employees perform
80. Quotes created in a graphical format and shared as an image
81. Advertisements (in papers, magazines, etc)
82. Photo contest results

Videos
83. Introduction to the company (could be by owner, employee or customer)
84. Customer testimonials
85. Product demonstration
86. How-to tips
87. Product or service recommendation
88. Funny story about your company, product or service
89. Video contest results

90. Powerpoint presentation
91. Interview of you
92. Interview where you interview an expert in your field
93. Interview where you interview a customer or key supplier
94. Make a funny video commercial about your business

High Tech and Business
95. New Gadget announcements
96. Product reviews
97. Interviews with high tech visionaries
98. Job Announcements
99. Career recommendations
100. Best places to work
101. Photos using a new gadget
102. Video demo of a new gadget
103. Video demo of using a software program, game or other computer "how to"
104. Pros and Cons lists
105. Business coaching tips
106. Legal tips

Money
107. Money management
108. Investment information
109. Current rates
110. Good deals that you find
111. Coupons that you find
112. Cost of living information
113. Price comparisons
114. Changing laws related to money or taxes
115. Wills, trusts and power of attorney tips
116. How to pick financial services or products
117. Success stories
118. Entrepreneurial advice
119. Money saving tips

Retirement
120. Planning for retirement
121. Reverse Mortgages
122. Travel for seniors

123. Senior discounts
124. AARP
125. Hobbies for seniors
126. Volunteer opportunities for seniors
127. Best places to eat for seniors
128. Fixed income funnies
129. Enjoying your grandchildren

Links
130. Links to relevant articles of interest to your target audience
131. Links to other people's videos
132. Links to products that you recommend
133. Links to websites that provide relevant information
134. Links to current or local events in your neighborhood

The following topics are intended to help you put the "social" in social media without revealing too much personal information.

Entertainment
135. Your favorite movie – quick review
136. Celebrity news
137. Sports results, events or appearances
138. Fashion likes or dislikes
139. Songs or music videos you like
140. Neighborhood events (art and wine festivals)
141. Favorite places to eat
142. Art shows
143. Theatrical performances and reviews
144. Book reviews
145. Movie reviews
146. Concert reviews
147. Recipe sharing
148. Party tips
149. Decorating ideas
150. Weather in your neck of the woods
151. Kids' sports events
152. Events at schools or churches
153. Wine lover's picks
154. Travel ideas
155. Travel reviews

Humor

156. Parenting humor
157. Industry specific humor
158. Clean jokes
159. Funny pictures of people
160. Funny pictures of animals
161. Funny pictures of sayings or quotes
162. "Friday Funny"
163. Funny videos you find on YouTube

Quotes

164. Industry quotes
165. Funny quotes
166. Law of Attraction quotes
167. Fashion quotes
168. Travel quotes
169. Sports quotes
170. Inspirational quotes
171. Success quotes
172. Political quotes
173. Parental quotes
174. Celebrity quotes
175. Quotes from books
176. Spiritual quotes

Trivia

177. Trivial facts about your industry
178. Trivial facts about your industry's demographic
179. Trivia about your product or service
180. Historical trivia
181. Sports trivia
182. Travel trivia
183. Business trivia
184. Kid trivia
185. Fashion trivia
186. Celebrity trivia
187. News trivia
188. Political trivia
189. Weather trivia

Food

190. How to prepare a recipe (video)
191. How to use a cooking technique *video)
192. Nutritional information
193. Entertaining ideas
194. Food trivia
195. Restaurant Reviews
196. Neighborhood hangouts
197. Coffee house reviews
198. Grilling ideas
199. Party menus
200. Food quotes
201. Photos of food that resemble something or someone

Do you get the idea? The breadth, depth and topic possibilities are only limited by your own imagination. Have fun!

Resources

When doing research on the Internet, it can be difficult to keep track of which piece of information came from which source. I did the best I could to track the sources, but in case I didn't give proper credit along the way, here is a list of websites where I found the majority of information.

www.thesocialskinny.com - by Cara Pring. She is awesome – her information is timely and she delivers it in a fun and sassy way.

www.business2community.com - a community of experts that deliver the latest trends, updates, webinars, whitepapers and everything else you can think of!

www.facebook.com - Did I mention I love Facebook?

www.emarketer.com - Lots of terrific information regarding the digital world.

www.socialmediaexaminer.com - I've taken many training webinars from Michael Stelzner. He is smart, current and easy to learn from. I am a certified blogger from the Social Media Examiner.

www.hubspot.com - A provider of Social Media tools, this site constantly has white papers and other great facts and information about social media.

www.kbjonline.com - My friend, Kate as mentioned in the Acknowledgements. A social media genius.

www.jobarnesonline.com - Jo keeps everything relevant and entertaining. If you ever need to know exactly what's going on with social media – check her out!

Many gurus out there have motivated, taught and inspired me. I enjoy following and learning from them!

Glossary of Terms

These are not all the terms that you will need to know to get more active in Social Media, but it's a place to start!

Avatar – a cartoon like image that represents a persona. These are often used for fun or in place of a regular personal photograph.

Blog – A form of on-line writing. There are all types of blogs, from personal journals, business journals, travel journals, business articles, how-tos and more.

Blogger – A person that uses a blog to communicate on the Internet.

Bookmarking – Websites that allow you to highlight and save (bookmark) your favorite sites and then share them with your network.

Business Page – Most of the Social Media platforms offer both a personal page and a business page. The business page does not share any personal profile information and you can write about and promote your business while keeping it separate. There are usually different analytics that go with a business page rather than a personal profile.

Channel – On YouTube, you can create your own "channel" whereby you can upload your own videos or collect other people's videos all in one place. You can also brand this page.

Chat – Also called "instant messaging". A means of communicating directly with someone in your own "chat room" while you're both on-line.

Circles – On Google+ you create your own "circles" of friends and acquaintances. It allows you to place your contacts into categories so that you can communicate with each category with the most appropriate content.

Clickstream – Analytics that track a users "click" on a website. Trackable features include which website a user clicked through rom and how they navigate your site.

CMS – Content Management System – the database and software behind building a website. For example, Wordpress is a CMS.

Content Marketing – A non-self promoting means of marketing. By providing content that is useful to the target customer, you build trust and loyalty. Items such as blogs, e-newsletters, special reports, social media, videos and Infographics are all examples of content marketing.

Comment – Most blogs, articles, Social Media platforms and many websites have a place where you, the reader, can make a comment. You can give feedback about what you read or add your own knowledge about a subject.

Connections – These are the people in your network that you follow and that follow you. When you post information, you are sharing it with your connections (depending upon your privacy settings).

Digg – A Social Bookmarking site that allows you to save your favorite websites and share them with your network.

Disqus – A commenting plugin that filters out SPAM on your website. It allows you to make your comment section more customized to your look and feel.

Delicious – A Social Bookmarking site that allows you to save your favorite websites and share them with your network.

Ebooks – Electronic publications (books) that you can view on your computer, tablet or phone.

Facebook – #1 Social Media platform with over 1 billion users worldwide

Facebook Apps – In order to do certain things on Facebook, you need an App(application) which someone developed. Examples include, contests, birthday reminders, games and surveys.

Facebook Group – A group is a section on Facebook where people of a certain interest or topic can mingle. As the group manager, you determine the privacy settings (public or private) and facilitate the conversations.

Facebook Notes – When you have more than just a few sentences to share or have a document you would like to share, you can use the "notes" feature on Facebook.

Fan Page – Also called a Business page. When Facebook first started, all business pages were called "fan pages". The term has stuck and many people still call the business page a fan page.

Flickr – A photo-sharing website where you can post your images and share them on a website or with your network.

Forum – Similar to groups, forums are created around a particular interest or topic. If you are the manager of the forum, you can control who views the conversations. Additionally, if you wish to join a forum, you may need to get permission from the forum manager.

Follow Friday (#ff) – On Twitter every Friday, people use the hash tag #FF and suggest to their network, people they should follow.

Foursquare – A location based Social platform whereby people can check into business establishments. They can share their location with friends, see who else is there and make comments about their experience at the business.

Google Alerts – A tool provided by Google to alert you when something is being shared or written about a topic that interests you. For example, you could set up a Google Alert with your name or your business name so that you can monitor what is being said about you (see Reputation Management also).

Google+ - A Social Media platform similar to Facebook but with some differing features.

Groups – Sites like LinkedIn and Facebook have groups. See Facebook Groups for a definition.

Hashtag – The # symbol represents a hashtag, which is a trending tool to let people on Twitter find additional information on a particular topic.

Hangout – On Google+, you can get a number of people in your network to "hang out" in a video chat room. You see all attendees on your screen like a video conference. This feature is good for virtual meetings, interviews, information sessions and just for fun!

Hootsuite – An automation tool where you can write and schedule posts on Social Media. You can also upload a file with bulk posts already written.

Inbound Marketing – Refers to advertising using Social Media, blogs, articles, content marketing and email.

Infographic – Visual story telling through the use of data and images. Facts are critical to Infographics as is an appealing, easy to understand format.

Instagram – A Social Media platform which uses photos or images as content.

Instant Messaging – See definition for "chat".

Keyword – Search engines such as Google and Bing use keywords to rank websites and content. So when someone uses a keyword, the most relevant sites appear at the top of the search page. Keywords are searchable from every Social Media platform, as well as articles, blogs and websites.

Klout – A company that offers a way to analyze a person's influence on their network. It uses analytics based upon how many shares, likes and other data to measure influence.

Likes – Whenever anyone posts something on Facebook, people in their network have the ability to "Like" it. Additionally, most websites now offer the ability to "Like" a page, post or photo, which links back to the person's Facebook profile. The more likes a post gets, the more people that see it.

LinkedIn – The #1 professional Social Media site where business people network and connect. Used for recruiting, sales leads and information sharing.

LinkedIn Groups – see definition for Facebook Groups

Lurker – When someone reads a page or posts without contributing to the conversation.

Manta – An on-line community strictly for businesses.

Meme – Trends and viral phenomenon that represent a cultural shift, pattern or phase.

MySpace – Social Media platform popular with artists and musicians.

Newsfeed – The section on Facebook where you read what's going on in your network. You can read what's happening and then comment or "like" or share it.

Opt-in – When you give someone permission to email you directly. Often you see these on social media where they offer you an incentive to provide your email address. By law, you must agree to receive emails or it is considered SPAM.

Organic – There are two types of "organic". One is where something you produce (such as an audio or video) has a "homegrown" feel to it, rather than polished and professional. The other is when something takes on a life of it's own and becomes "viral" without any action by you.

Pin – The act of sharing something on your own profile (or board) on Pinterest.

Pinterest –A photo sharing Social Media website.

Plaxo – A Social Media community site for businesses.

Plugin – A feature that you can use to add certain functionality on a Wordpress website. For example, if you'd like to have a fancy photo gallery, there's a plugin for that!

Post – Sharing content on Social Media. For example, when you provide a status update on Facebook, you are "posting" your status.

Poke – A Social Media app on Facebook that allows you to give a virtual poke to a friend.

Podcast – An audio training program or interview.

Privacy Settings – Each Social Media site has a setting whereby you can control who views your content. Choices might include particular lists of people, such as friends, acquaintences, business network and family. The setting that allows anyone, anywhere to view our content is "public".

Reddit – Self named "The Front Page of the Internet" is a bookmarking site where people submit content and it gets ranked according to popularity.

Reputation Management – With the internet being so vast, it is difficult to know everything people are saying about you. Some people may write slanderous or inappropriate things and cause your on-line reputation to suffer. Or perhaps you had a run in with the law or a pending lawsuit. You will need to become well versed in managing your own reputation on-line.

Retweet – When something you've tweeted on Twitter gets shared with another person's Twitter followers.

RSS – Real Simple Syndication. This refers to automatic sharing (or syndication) of your articles, blogs or website content.

Screencast – A video or live event whereby viewers watch you perform something on your computer screen.

SEO – Search Engine Optimization – The use of specific tools and techniques for getting the highest ranking when someone searches your key words.

Share – Forwarding content or posts that you like to your network. This can be on Facebook or on any website that is set up with sharing ability.

Skype – A free video conferencing tool that utilizes computer video cameras and the Internet.

SlideShare – A website where you can upload presentations (PowerPoint or Keynote or other presentation generating software) for viewers to see.

SMO – Social Media Optimization – See SEO – using similar techniques as SEO but focused on Social Media Content

StumbleUpon – An Internet assistant that propagates content based upon what you like.

Tag Cloud – A feature on a blog that has key words. You can click on a key word in a tag cloud to go to all the blog posts that relate to that topic.

Technorati – A search engine specific to blogs. You can submit your blog to be searched on Technorati.

Thumbnail – An image that fits in a small square. Often the size that is used in a social media profile.

Timeline – A feature on Facebook, which lets you scroll to different dates on your profile page. It sorts your posts based upon the date shared.

Trend – Whatever is hot for the moment on Social Media, with a large emphasis on Twitter (Twitter Trend).

Tweet – the content that is shared on a Twitter account. Tweets are considered a "micro blog" post and must fit within 140 characters or less.

Tweetup – An event where people that have met and communicate on Twitter meet in person.

Twitter – A Social Media platform for micro-blogging information, personal comments, sharing links and advertising.

Twitter Chat – Using a particular hashtag (#) with a key word to generate a conversation on Twitter. Those who participate in the chat follow it by following the hashtag being used.

Tumblr – A free blog hosting site for personal or professional blogs.

Viddler – A video streaming service for businesses

Viral Marketing – Like a virus, marketing that grows on its own by being shared rapidly and to a wide audience.

Vlog – Video blogging. This can be done on a regular blog or website.

Web Analytics – The ability to track what kind of activity happens on the Internet. For example, how many visitors to a website, how long a visitor viewed the site, what pages they viewed, etc. An example of a tool to measure web analytics, is Google Analytics.

Webinar – An on-line training session using video conference meeting tools, such as GoToMeeting.com

Widget – A Wordpress tool, which places content in the sidebar or footer of a blog page.

Wiki – A website that allows users to add or edit content.

Wikipedia – An on-line encyclopedia in which anyone can contribute.

Wordpress – A CMS (Content Management System) used to design websites. Originally started for bloggers, it has full feature functionality to create whatever website you want. It is also a free platform, you just need a domain and hosting accounts.

YouTube – A Social Media platform that strictly uses video. Owned by Google.

Yammer – A professional, private Social Media platform to be used within a company.

Yelp – Location based Social Media platform and review site. You can check in at a business and share it with your network. You can also review the business and share that as well.

@Mention – A code that is trackable when someone refers to another person on Twitter. For example, you can check to see who has mentioned you and in what context through your Twitter account. In addition if you wish to reference someone in regards to something they shared or said, you use the @ before their Twitter handle.

About The Author

Claudia Loens, Founder of Wordflirt, is a Social Media Content Producer, Recruiting Consultant, Writer, Trainer, Coach and Mom. She designs Wordpress websites for her clients, as well as, helps them develop social media and traditional marketing programs. Her passion is to help small to mid-sized businesses and Recruiting teams grow their bottom line by using GREAT social media content.

A native to Northern California, she is well traveled and has a passion for tropical beaches. Married and mother of four daughters, she spends a lot of her time in the kitchen and in the car! The mobility of writing and social media allows her to be an active mom and still enjoy a great business.

In addition to this book, she is also the author of "Believe in Love" (a romance novel on Amazon) and "Happily Hired" (a non-fiction guide to helping job seekers land their perfect job). She writes poetry, journals and blogs whenever she can.

Visit her at www.wordflirtsocialmedia.com to learn more about how she helps companies grow. You can also obtain a printable copy of the worksheets on her website.

NOTES

NOTES